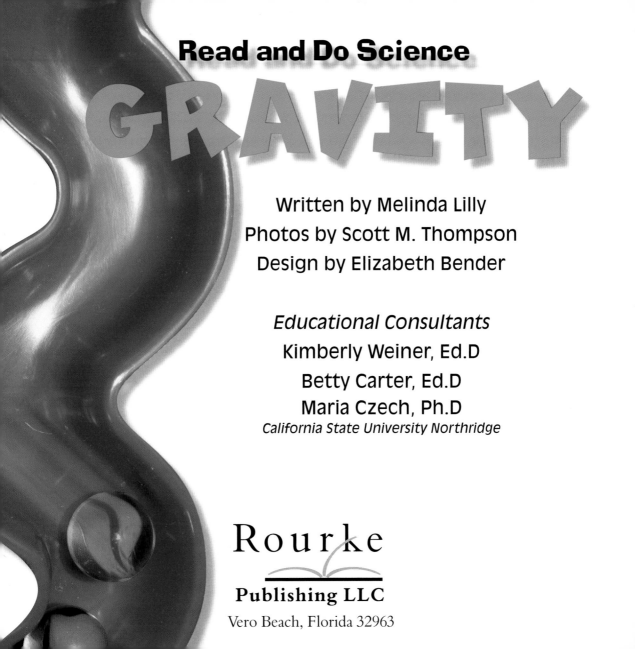

Read and Do Science
GRAVITY

Written by Melinda Lilly

Photos by Scott M. Thompson

Design by Elizabeth Bender

Educational Consultants

Kimberly Weiner, Ed.D

Betty Carter, Ed.D

Maria Czech, Ph.D
California State University Northridge

Rourke
Publishing LLC

Vero Beach, Florida 32963

Before You Read This Book

Think about these facts:

1. In space, if you jump you will keep going in the same direction. On Earth, if you jump you will fall back down. Why do you think this happens?

2. Predict which would fall faster, a bowling ball or a parachute.

The experiments in this book should be undertaken with adult supervision.

For Bridge Street Elementary

—S. T.

©2004 Rourke Publishing LLC

Library of Congress Cataloging-in-Publication Data

ISBN 1-58952-642-2

Printed in the USA

Table of Contents

Jump up!

When you jump up, **gravity** makes you come back down. It pulls everything on Earth down, toward the center of our planet.

Gravity isn't strong enough to pull you under the ground. However, it is strong enough to pull you back down to the ground when you jump up.

To slow the speed of gravity's downward tug on us, we use a force called **drag**. Drag pulls in the opposite direction that something is moving.

A **parachute** uses drag to fall slowly.

Toy Parachute

What You Need:

- 24-inch (60.96-cm*) paper square
- Tape
- Hole punch
- 96 inches (2.44 meters) of string
- Open-weave plastic basket
  (strawberries are sold in these)
- Toy

* cm is short for centimeter

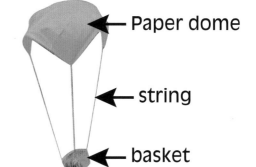

Paper dome

string

basket

Tape all corners of the paper square.

Slide a taped corner into the hole punch. Have an adult help you punch a hole in the taped corner.

Punch holes in the other corners.

Stretch the string along the ruler.

Pinch the string at the 6-inch (15.24-cm) mark and pull it to the start of the ruler. That doubles the string's length.

Do it twice more. Now you have measured 6 inches (15.24 cm), four times.

Inches	Centimet
0	0
	1
	2
1	3
	4
2	5
	6
	7
3	8
	9
4	10
	11
	12
5	13
	14
6	15

6 inches x 4 = 24 inches

15.24 cm x 4 = 60.96 cm

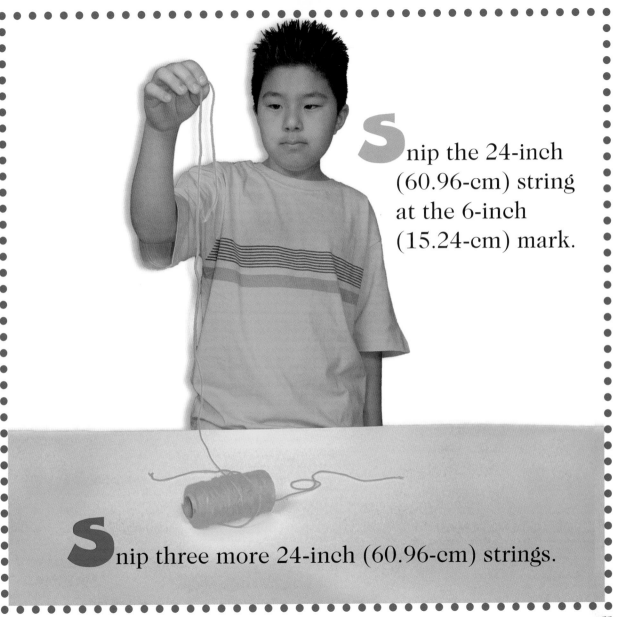

Snip the 24-inch (60.96-cm) string at the 6-inch (15.24-cm) mark.

Snip three more 24-inch (60.96-cm) strings.

Knot each string through one of the holes.

Tie each string to a different corner of the basket.

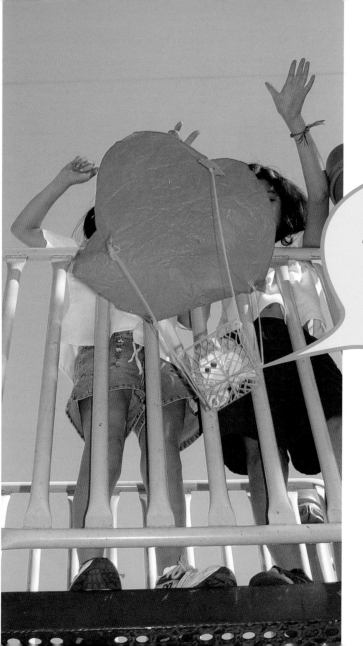

Place a toy in the basket.

I want my mommy!

Lift the parachute over your head. Drop it. Count how long it takes to reach the ground.

Drop the toy by itself. Count as it falls.

What goes up must come down!

Does it fall faster than with the parachute?

Why does the parachute slow the toy's fall?

As the parachute falls, it traps air inside its dome. The trapped air pushes against the inside of the dome. This increases drag and slows the fall.

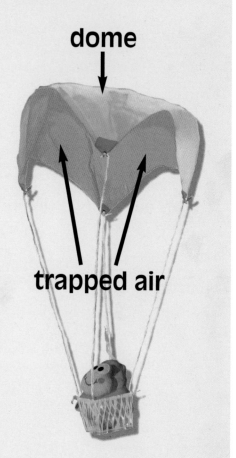

dome

trapped air

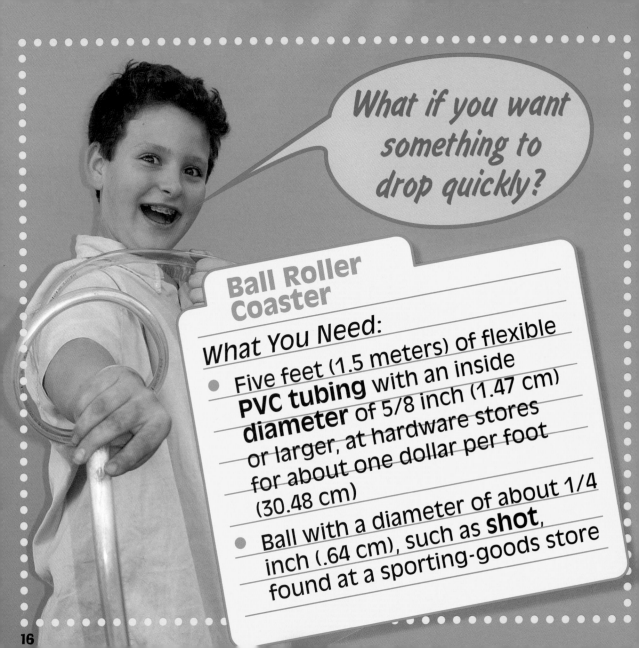

What if you want something to drop quickly?

Ball Roller Coaster

What You Need:

- Five feet (1.5 meters) of flexible **PVC tubing** with an inside **diameter** of 5/8 inch (1.47 cm) or larger, at hardware stores for about one dollar per foot (30.48 cm)

- Ball with a diameter of about 1/4 inch (.64 cm), such as **shot**, found at a sporting-goods store

Loop the tube.

Drop the ball into the top of the tube.

What can you do to the tube to help the ball zip zip zip zip zip zip zip zip zip zip zip zip zip zip zip zip zip zip zip zip zip around the loop?

To loop the loop, the ball has to go fast. Curve the tube steeply downward into the loop to make the ball go faster.

Gravity pulls the ball. It gives it enough **momentum,** or forward motion, to go around the loop.

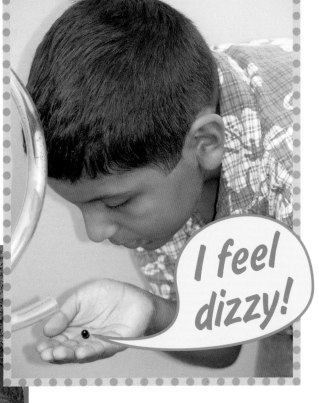

Shape the tube in different ways and set the ball racing.

The Lowdown on Gravity

Gravity pulls everything toward the center of Earth. Drag pulls against gravity. The straighter and steeper the drop, the faster the ball will roll.

That's what makes roller coasters fun!

Glossary

diameter (dy AM ih ter) — a line that passes through the center of a circle and touches it on both sides

drag (DRAG) — a force or power that resists movement

gravity (GRAV ih tea) — the force that attracts things to the Earth's center

momentum (mow MEN tum) — speed and power of motion

parachute (PAR uh shoot) — an umbrellalike object with cords that uses air resistance to slow its fall

PVC tubing (PVC TOO bing) — a plastic tube, flexible PVC tubing is used as piping for fountains and pools

shot (SHOT) — a small metal ball

Turn yourself into a roller coaster!
Wrap the tube around your arm.
What happens to the speed of
the ball if you lift your arm?
Can you make the ball go
back and forth?

Think About It!

1. Can you predict what would happen if you used a smaller parachute, maybe only half the size? With less drag, would the toy fall faster or slower?

2. What do you think would happen if you put a baseball in the basket? Predict whether it would fall faster or slower than an empty basket.

3. Gravity and the sloping tube cause the ball to roll. What do you think the effect on the ball would be if there was no gravity?

Index